Mosaic Tile Quilts

by Patricia Sanabria-Friederich

9 quilting projects inspired by the beautiful, historic mosaic tile floors of Costa Rica

Landauer Publishing, LLC

Mosaic Tile Quilts

by Patricia Sanabria-Friederich

This book was designed, produced, and published
by Landauer Publishing, LLC
3100 101st Street, Urbandale, IA 50322
800-557-2144; 515-287-2144; www.landauerpub.com

President/Publisher: Jeramy Lanigan Landauer
Vice President of Sales and Administration: Kitty Jacobson
Editor: Jeri Simon
Art Director: Laurel Albright
Technical Editor: Rhonda Matus
Quilt Photography: Sue Voegtlin

This book is printed on acid-free paper.

Printed in the United States 10 9 8 7 6 5 4 3 2 1

Library of Congress Control Number: 2013944446

ISBN 13: 978-1935726-46-3

Contents

About the Author

I grew up in Costa Rica where my love for sewing began at an early age. My grandmother was the first person to put a needle in my hand. She had a sewing machine cover and I was intrigued by the many small pieces of fabric that had been stitched together to create it. Sadly, my grandmother passed away before she could teach me how to make that sewing machine cover.

My sister and I were always in our mother's sewing room. We would play and make clothes and little blankets for our dolls while she sewed. I was very fortunate that the school I attended had sewing classes beginning in the first grade. While I was learning many important lessons at school, my mother was helping me and my sister with our hand sewing and embroidery assignments at home.

Today I live in Cedarburg, Wisconsin, where I am married to my wonderful husband Doyle. He has been by my side supporting me on my quilting journey since the first quilt I ever made. We have two grown sons, Steve and Nick, who received two of my first quilts. It is always fun to show them what I am working on when they come home to visit.

I am part owner in our family's quilt and fabric shop. My sister Sandra, brother Mario and I own the shop located in San Joaquin De Flores, Herdia, Costa Rica. The shop, El Baul De Mi Abuelita, is named in honor of our grandmother. The shop name translates to "My Grandmother's Trunk".

I am truly blessed by my family and friends.

Patricia Sanabria-Friederich

Quilts and Tiles
Creating quilts from mosaic tiles

I was sitting in church with my mother in my hometown of San Joaquin de Flores, Costa Rica, when I looked down and realized the mosaic floor pattern would be ideal for a quilt. I went back later to take some photographs for reference when making the quilt pattern. As I began adapting the mosaic floor into a quilt, the idea of creating more quilts from different places in Costa Rica struck me and the idea for this book was born.

The quilts in this book were inspired by mosaic tile floors found in Costa Rican churches, schools and homes. The floors follow the mosaic tile tradition used in Europe. Up until the mid-to-late 1800's tiles were imported from Europe, but by the early 1900's Costa Rican craftsmen began creating and designing their own tiles. As tile factories began to open in Costa Rica, more people were able to afford to have these beautiful mosaics in their homes. However, the pigments and molds still came from Europe and the more colorful or complex the design,

the more expensive the tile. Thus, there was a correlation between the tile design and the social status of the owner. The building's floor patterns reflect what was in fashion at the time of construction. By the 1940's, mosaic tile floors began to fall out of fashion and were used less and less in newer construction. Some of the tile floor colors have faded over time, especially in buildings more than 70-80 years old. To this day Costa Rica's handmade mosaics tiles are still produced for people who want to keep the traditional-style floors.

Right: The tile in the San Joaquin de Flores Church in the author's hometown of San Joaquin de Flores, Herdia, Costa Rica, became the inspiration for her first mosaic tile quilt.

I believe there are many similarities between traditional mosaic tile floors and quilts. The tile artist and the quilter both create using molds or patterns while paying special attention to color combinations and lines. Tile floors and quilts are often put together using a four-block design.

Top: The mosaic tile floor in the San Joaquin de Flores Church that inspired the San Joaquin Quilt pictured below.

The tradition of mosaic tile design is to create floor patterns when tiles are laid side by side. Coordinating border tiles, which create a rug-like design, often surround the floor pattern. However, a solid color tile may be used to create the floor's border, similar to how we border our quilts.

Tile and quilt makers construct their masterpieces in three layers. Adding colors to a sectioned dye mold creates the mosaic tile. This step relates to a quilter's first layer of piecing. The tile maker then adds the second and third layers of cement prior to the tile being pressed. A quilter uses batting and backing as the second and third layers of her quilt. These three pieces are then quilted.

San Joaquin Quilt

There are a multitude of mosaic floor designs that can be converted into quilts using fabric and piecing or appliqué techniques. These can be found in historic and public buildings, homes and churches throughout the world. What a wonderful way to honor the many men who spent hours creating the beautiful floors we walk on every day.

Basilica of Santo Domingo Heredia

Santo Domingo is located approximately seven kilometers from Costa Rica's capital city of San Jose. It is a primarily Catholic town influenced by the nineteenth century economics and architecture of San Jose.

As the community of Santo Domingo grew it became apparent another church was needed to help out the existing Church of El Rosario. Between the efforts of the local community and Church of El

Rosario's priest, Father Benito Saenz-Reyes, the money was raised to build another church. The new church, Basilica of Santo Domingo, was built between 1879 and 1891 with neocolonial influence and neoclassical style. The Basilica opened on July 23, 1891, and became the main church (parroquia) of Santo Domingo.

The mosaic tiles that grace the Basilica of Santo Domingo floors have no clear record of origin. While the designs are beautiful and elegant, the colors are conservative. One well-known

piece of the church's history is the church bells. The bells, La Bernarda and La Dominga, were named in honor of Monsignor Bernardo Thiel and Saint Santo Domingo, for whom the town was also named.

Basilica of Santo Domingo Heredia was declared a national heritage by the government of Costa Rica on January 8, 2013. The Church continues to fulfill its functions and Catholic services to this day.

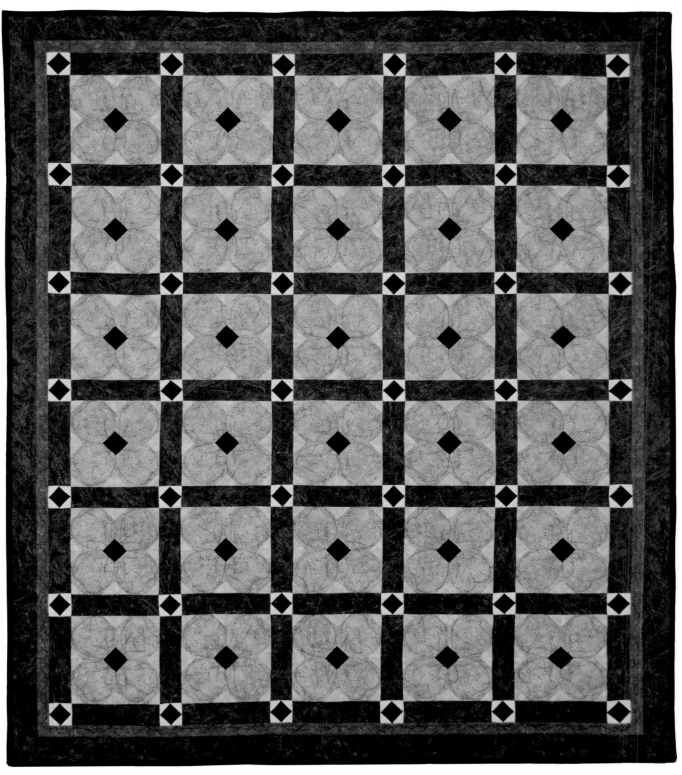

Santo Domingo Quilt

Santo Domingo Quilt

Finished quilt size: 52" x 60-3/4"

Finished block sizes:
7" x 7" and 1-3/4" x 1-3/4"

Materials

1-1/2 yards dark beige fabric
3/4 yard gold fabric
1 yard black fabric
1/4 yard light beige fabric
1-1/2 yards blue fabric
1/3 yard brown fabric
3-1/4 yards backing fabric
58" x 67" batting

Quantities are for 40/44"-wide, 100% cotton fabrics. Measurements include 1/4" seam allowances. Sew with right sides together unless otherwise stated.

Cut the Fabrics

From dark beige fabric, cut:

- 12—4" x 42" strips.
  From the strips, cut:
  120—4" squares for Block 1.

From gold fabric, cut:

- 13—1-1/2" x 42" strips.
  From the strips, cut:
  360—1-1/2" squares for Block 1.

From black fabric, cut:

- 5—1-1/2" x 42" strips.
  From the strips, cut:
  120—1-1/2" squares for Block 1.
- 2—1-3/4" x 42" strips.
  From the strips, cut:
  42—1-3/4" center squares
  for Block 2.
- 6—2-1/2" x 42" binding strips.
  Sew the strips together to make one long strip.

From light beige fabric, cut:

- 4—1-3/4" x 42" strips.
  From the strips, cut:
  84—1-3/4" squares. Cut each square in half diagonally for a total of 168 triangles for Block 2.

From blue fabric, cut:

- 15—2-1/4" x 42" strips.
  From the strips, cut:
  71—2-1/4" x 7-1/2" sashing rectangles.
- 6—2-1/2" x 42" strips
  for outer border.

From brown fabric, cut:

- 6—1-1/2" x 42" strips
  for inner border.

From backing fabric, cut:

- 2—34" x 58" rectangles.

Block 1 Assembly

1. Draw a diagonal line on the wrong side of the (360) 1-1/2" gold squares and the (120) 1-1/2" black squares.

2. Referring to the diagram, place a 1-1/2" gold square on a corner of a 4" dark beige square, right sides together. Sew on the drawn line. Trim 1/4" beyond the stitching line. Press open to reveal a triangle.

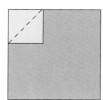 

3. Refer to step 2 to add (1) 1-1/2" black square and (2) 1-1/2" gold squares to the remaining corners to complete a snowball unit. Make 120 snowball units.

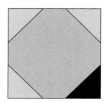

Make 120

4. Lay out 4 snowball units as shown. Join into rows; join rows to complete the block. The block should measure 7-1/2" square. Make 30 Block 1.

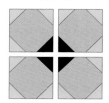 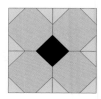

Make 30

Block 2 Assembly

1. Sew (2) 1-3/4" light beige triangles to opposite sides of a 1-3/4" black center square. Press seams toward triangles.

2. Sew (2) 1-3/4" light beige triangles to the remaining sides of the black center square. Press seams toward triangles. If necessary, trim the block to 2-1/4" square. Make 42 Block 2.

Make 42

Quilt Center Assembly

1. Referring to the Quilt Center Assembly Diagram, lay out 30 Block 1, 42 Block 2 and (71) 2-1/4" x 7-1/2" blue sashing rectangles in rows as shown.

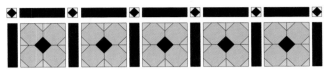

2. Sew the pieces together in rows. You will have (7) Block 2/sashing rectangle rows and (6) Block 1/sashing rectangle rows. Press the seams in each row toward the sashing strips.

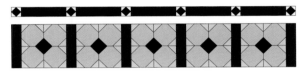

3. Join the rows to make the quilt center. Press seams in one direction.

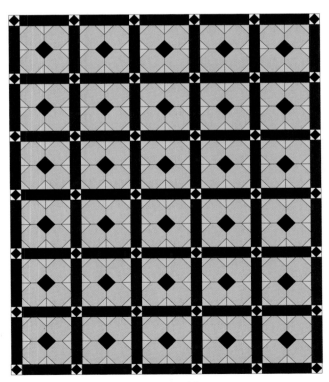

Quilt Center Assembly Diagram

Adding the Inner Border

1. Piece the 1-1/2" x 42" brown inner border strips together into one long strip. From the strip, cut (2) 1-1/2" x 46" top/bottom inner border strips and (2) 1-1/2" x 54-3/4" side inner border strips.

2. Sew the top/bottom inner border strips to the top and bottom edges of the quilt center. Press seams toward inner border.

3. Sew the side inner border strips to the sides of the quilt center. Press seams toward inner border.

Adding the Outer Border

1. Piece the 2-1/2" x 42" blue outer border strips together into one long strip. From the strip, cut (2) 2-1/2" x 48-1/2" top/bottom outer border strips and (2) 2-1/2" x 60-1/2" side outer border strips.

2. Sew the top/bottom outer border strips to the top and bottom edges of the quilt top. Press seams toward outer border.

3. Sew the side outer border strips to the sides of the quilt top. Press seams toward outer border.

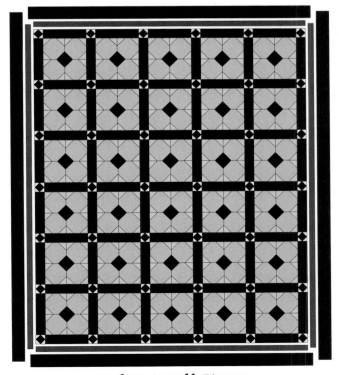

Quilt Top Assembly Diagram

13

Complete the Quilt

1. Sew the 34" x 58" backing rectangles together along one long edge, using a 1/2" seam allowance. Press the seam allowance open. Seam will run horizontally across quilt.

2. Layer the quilt top, batting and pieced backing together.

3. Quilt the layers together.

4. Attach the binding to the outside edges to finish the quilt.

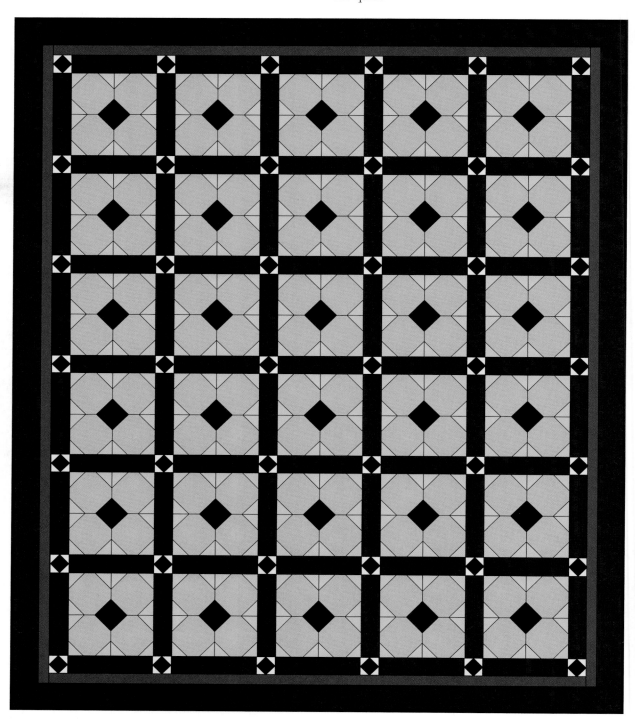

Santo Domingo Quilt

52" x 60-3/4"

Santo Domingo Wallhanging

Santo Domingo Wallhanging

Finished wallhanging size:
49-1/4" x 49-1/4"

Finished block sizes:
10" square and 3" square

Materials

3/8 yard blue fabric
5/8 yard white fabric
1-1/4 yards brown fabric
1 yard red fabric
3/4 yard black fabric
7/8 yard beige fabric
1/4 yard gold fabric
Paper-backed fusible web (optional)
3-1/8 yards backing fabric
56" x 56" batting

Quantities are for 40/44"-wide, 100% cotton fabrics. Measurements include 1/4" seam allowances. Sew with right sides together unless otherwise stated.

Cut the Fabrics

Note: Label the fabric pieces and place in stacks as you are cutting.

From blue fabric, cut:

- 1—3-3/4" x 42" strip.
  From the strip, cut:
  4—3-3/4" squares. Cut each square diagonally in an X for a total of 16 A triangles for Block 1.
- 3—2-3/8" x 42" strips.
  From the strips, cut:
  36—2-3/8" F squares for Block 3.

From white fabric, cut:

- 1—3-3/4" x 42" strip.
  From the strip, cut:
  8—3-3/4" squares. Cut each square diagonally in an X for a total of 32 A triangles for Block 1.

- 3—2-3/8" x 42" strips.
  From the strips, cut:
  36—2-3/8" F squares for Block 3.
- 3—1-1/2" x 42" strips for Block 2.

From brown fabric, cut:

- 4—3-1/8" x 42" strips.
  From the strips, cut:
  2—3-1/8" x 33-1/2" strips and 2—3-1/8" x 38-3/4" strips for Border 3.
- 2—3" x 42" strips.
  From the strips, cut:
  16—3" D squares for Block 1.
- 1—3-3/4" x 42" strip.
  From the strip, cut:
  4—3-3/4" squares. Cut each square diagonally in an X for a total of 16 A triangles for Block 1.
- 1—1-3/4" x 42" strip.
  From the strip, cut:
  16—1-3/4" x 3" C rectangles for Block 1.
- 4—1-1/2" x 42" strips.
  From the strips, cut:
  2—1-1/2" x 29-1/2" strips and 2—1-1/2" x 31-1/2" strips for Border 1.
- 5—1-1/2" x 42" strips for Border 5.

From red fabric, cut:

- 1—4-3/4" x 42" strip.
  From the strip, cut:
  4—4-3/4" I squares for Border 4.
- 6—2-1/2" x 42" binding strips.
- 7—1-1/2" x 42" strips.
  From the strips, cut:
  2—1-1/2" x 31-1/2" strips and 2—1-1/2" x 33-1/2" strips for Border 2.
  Set aside 3 strips for Block 2.

From black fabric, cut:

- 3—3-1/2" x 42" strips.
  From the strips, cut:
  12—3-1/2" x 10-1/2" sashing rectangles.
- 1—3" x 42" strip.
  From the strip, cut:
  4—3" D squares for Block 1.
- 4—2" x 42" strips.
  From the strips, cut:
  72—2" G squares for Block 3.

From beige fabric, cut:

- 3—5-1/2" x 42" strips.
  From the strips, cut:
  20—5-1/2" squares. Cut each square diagonally in an X for a total of 80 H triangles for Border 4.
- 5—1-3/4" x 42" strips.
  From the strips, cut:
  16—1-3/4" x 4-1/4" E rectangles, 16—1-3/4" x 3" C rectangles and 32—1-3/4" B squares for Block 1.

From backing fabric, cut:

- 2—28-1/2" x 56" rectangles.

Block 1 Assembly

1. Lay out 2 white A triangles, 1 blue A triangle and 1 brown A triangle as shown. Sew the triangles together in pairs. Press seams toward darker triangles. Sew the pairs together to complete 1 Hourglass Unit. Make 16 Hourglass Units.

Make 16

2. Draw a diagonal line from corner to corner on the wrong side of (32) 1-3/4" beige B squares.

3. Referring to the diagram, place a beige B square on a brown C rectangle, right sides together. Sew on the drawn line. Trim 1/4" beyond the sewn line. Press open to reveal a triangle. Repeat by placing a beige B square at the opposite end of the brown rectangle to complete 1 Flying Geese Unit. Make 16 Flying Geese Units.

Make 16

4. Lay out 4 Hourglass Units, 4 Flying Geese Units, 4 brown D squares, 1 black D square, 4 beige E rectangles and 4 beige C rectangles as shown. Sew the pieces together in rows. Press seams toward D squares and Flying Geese Units.

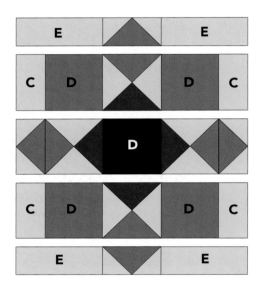

5. Sew the rows together. Press seams toward rows with brown D squares. Make 4.

Make 4

6. Trace 4 of the appliqué pattern on page 22. Cut and prepare the appliqué pieces from the gold fabric using the appliqué method of your choice. Follow the manufacturer's instructions if using paper-backed fusible web.

7. Center an appliqué shape on each block's black D square, using the block diagram as a guide. Appliqué the shape in place using your favorite method. Needle-turn appliqué was used along the edges of each of the appliqué pieces in the quilt. Make 4 Block 1.

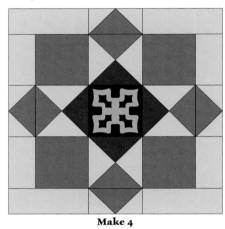

Make 4

Block 2 Assembly

1. Sew 2 white 1-1/2" x 42" strips and 1 red 1-1/2" x 42" strip together to make Strip Set 1 as shown. Press seams toward the red strip. Cut strip set into 18—1-1/2"-wide Segment 1.

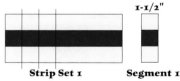

Strip Set 1   **Segment 1**

2. Sew 2 red 1-1/2" x 42" strips and 1 white 1-1/2" x 42" strip together to make Strip Set 2 as shown. Press seams toward the red strips. Cut strip set into 9—1-1/2"-wide Segment 2.

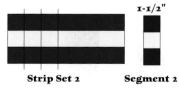

Strip Set 2   **Segment 2**

3. Sew 2 Segment 1 and 1 Segment 2 together to make Block 2 as shown. Press seams open. Make 9 Block 2.

Make 9

Block 3 Assembly

1. With right sides together, layer a white F square and a blue F square. Draw a diagonal line from corner to corner on the wrong side of the white square.

2. Sew 1/4" on both sides of the drawn line. Cut on the drawn line. Press seam toward the blue triangle. The half-square triangles should measure 2" square. Repeat Steps 1 – 2 to make 72 half-square triangles.

Make 72

3. Lay out 2 half-square triangles and 2 black G squares as shown. Sew into rows; press seams toward black squares. Join rows to complete Block 3. Block should measure 3-1/2" square. Make 36 Block 3.

Make 36

Wallhanging Center Assembly

1. Referring to the Wallhanging Center Assembly Diagram, lay out 4 Block 1, 9 Block 2 and 12 black 3-1/2" x 10-1/2" sashing rectangles as shown.

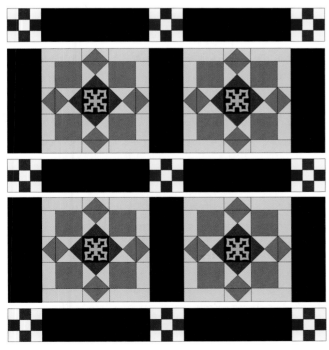

Wallhanging Center Assembly Diagram

2. Sew the pieces together in each Block 2/sashing row and each sashing/Block 1 row. Press seams toward the sashing.

3. Join the rows to make the wallhanging center. Press seams in one direction.

Adding the Borders

1. Sew the brown 1-1/2" x 29-1/2" Border 1 strips to the top and bottom of the quilt center. Sew the brown 1-1/2" x 31-1/2" Border 1 strips to the remaining sides of the wallhanging center. Press all seams toward Border 1.

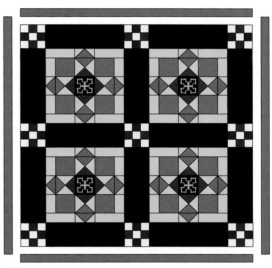

Wallhanging Top Assembly Diagram

2. Sew the red 1-1/2" x 31-1/2" Border 2 strips to the top and bottom of the wallhanging top. Sew the red 1-1/2" x 33-1/2" Border 2 strips to the remaining sides of the wallhanging top. Press all seams toward Border 2.

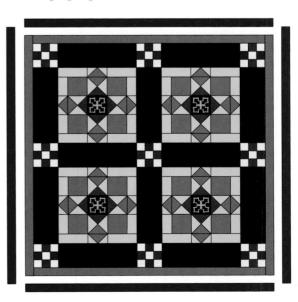

19

3. Sew the brown 3-1/8" x 33-1/2" Border 3 strips to the top and bottom of the wallhanging top. Sew the brown 3-1/8" x 38-3/4" Border 3 strips to the remaining sides of the wallhanging top. Press all seams toward Border 3.

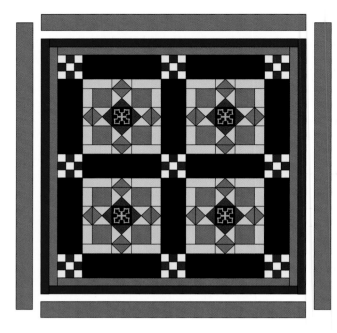

4. Sew beige H triangles to opposite edges of each Block 3 to make a Block-Triangle Unit as shown. Press seams toward triangles. Make 36 Block-Triangle Units.

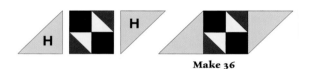

Make 36

5. Sew 9 Block-Triangle Units together in a strip; press seams in one direction. Add a beige H triangle to each end. Trim the strip 1/4" beyond the point of the top and bottom blocks to complete Border 4 strip. Make 4 Border 4 strips. Each strip should measure 4-3/4" x 38-3/4".

Make 4

6. Sew 2 Border 4 strips to opposite edges of the wallhanging top. Press seams toward Border 3.

7. Sew a red 4-3/4" I square to each end of remaining Border 4 strips. Press seams toward squares. Add these to remaining edges of wallhanging top. Press seams toward Border 3.

8. Sew the brown 1-1/2" x 42" Border 5 strips together. Cut the sewn strip into 2—1-1/2" x 47-1/4" border strips and 2—1-1/2" x 49-1/4" border strips.

9. Sew the 1-1/2" x 47-1/4" border strips to the top and bottom edges of the wallhanging top. Sew the 1-1/2" x 49-1/4" border strips to the remaining sides of the wallhanging top. Press all seams toward Border 5.

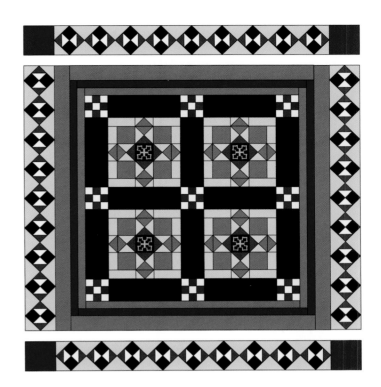

Complete the Wallhanging

1. Sew the 28-1/2" x 56" backing rectangles together along one long edge, using a 1/2" seam allowance. Press the seam allowance open.

2. Layer wallhanging top, batting and pieced backing.

3. Quilt as desired.

4. Bind with red binding strips.

Appliqué Pattern

Santo Domingo Wallhanging

49-1/4" x 49-1/4"

Cartago House

This unassuming house, located in the city of Cartago approximately 24 kilometers from San Jose and in the slopes of Irazu volcano, was built around 1910 out of wood. It is believed the home's tile floors were hand crafted locally.

The city of Cartago is an important part of Costa Rica's history. It was home to the first Spanish families and governors who relocated from Spain. After independence from Spain in 1821 Cartago became Costa Rica's first capital. However, during 1822 and 1823 the capital moved between the cities of Cartago, San Jose and Alajuela. In 1823 it was decided Cartago would be the capital of Costa Rica. This did not last and after a short civil war San Jose was named the capital and remains so to this day.

Cartago was also the site of the first Permanent International Rights Court and the first International Court for the Human Rights. It was built by

donations from Andrew Carnegie and inaugurated in 1908. In 1911, the building was destroyed by an earthquake and the court was moved to San Jose. Cartago has a strong religious history and the Basilica de Nuestra Señora de Los Angeles, named after the patron Saint of Costa Rica, is located there.

Cartago Table Runner

Cartago Table Runner

Finished runner size: 14-1/4" x 42"

Materials

1/2 yard red print fabric
1/4 yard gold print fabric
2/3 yard green fabric
1-1/3 yards backing fabric
Template plastic
21" x 48" batting

Quantities are for 40/44"-wide, 100% cotton fabrics. Measurements include 1/4" seam allowances. Sew with right sides together unless otherwise stated.

Note: Patterns for Templates A, B and C are on pages 30.

Cut the Fabrics

From red print fabric, cut:
- 3 Template A.
- 2 Template B reversed.
- 3—2-1/2" x 42" binding strips.

From gold print fabric, cut:
- 8 Template B.

From green fabric, cut:
- 8 Template C.
- 3—2-3/4" x 42" strips.
  From the strips, cut:
  2—2-3/4" x 37-1/2" and
  2—2-3/4" x 14-1/4" border strips.

Note: Borders are exact length needed. You may want to cut them longer to allow for differences in piecing.

From backing fabric, cut:
- 1—21" x 48" rectangle.

Table Runner Center Assembly

1. Referring to the Table Runner Center Assembly Diagram, lay out 3 red print A pieces, 2 red print B reversed pieces, 8 gold print B pieces and 8 green C pieces in diagonal rows as shown.

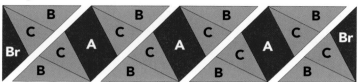

Table Runner Center Assembly Diagram

2. Sew the pieces together in diagonal rows. Press seams away from the green C pieces.

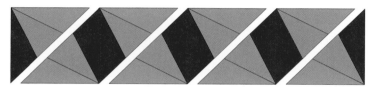

3. Join the diagonal rows to make the table runner center. Press seams in one direction.

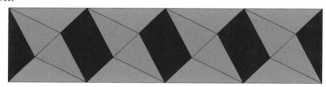

Adding the Border

1. Referring to the Table Runner Top Assembly Diagram, sew the green 2-3/4" x 37-1/2" border strips to the long edges of the table runner center. Press seams toward border.

2. Sew the green 2-3/4" x 14-1/4" border strips to the remaining edges of the table runner center. Press seams toward border.

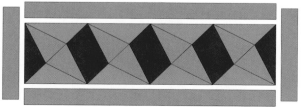

Table Runner Top Assembly Diagram

Complete the Table Runner

1. Layer table runner top, batting and backing.

2. Quilt as desired.

3. Bind with red binding strips.

Cartago Wallhanging

Cartago Wallhanging

Finished wallhanging size:
34-1/4" x 43-1/2"

Materials

3/4 yard red fabric
1 yard blue fabric
1-1/4 yards light beige fabric
1-3/8 yards backing fabric
Template plastic
41" x 50" batting
   Quantities are for 40/44"-wide, 100% cotton fabrics. Measurements include 1/4" seam allowances. Sew with right sides together unless otherwise stated.
Note: Patterns for Templates A, B and C are on pages 30.

Cut the Fabrics

From red fabric, cut:
• 9 Template A.
• 6 Template B reversed.

From blue fabric, cut:
• 8 Template A reversed.
• 8 Template B.
• 5—2-1/2" x 42" binding strips.

From light beige fabric, cut:
• 24 Template C.
• 4—3-1/2" x 42" strips.
   From the strips, cut:
   2—3-1/2" x 37-1/2" and
   2—3-1/2" x 34-1/4" border strips.
Note: Borders are exact length needed. You may want to cut them longer to allow for differences in piecing.

Wallhanging Center Assembly

1. Referring to Wallhanging Center Assembly Diagram, lay out 9 red A pieces, 6 red B reversed pieces, 8 blue A reversed pieces, 8 blue B pieces and 24 light beige C pieces in diagonal rows as shown.

2. Sew the pieces together in diagonal rows. Press seams away from the light beige C pieces.

3. Join the diagonal rows to make the wallhanging center. Press seams in one direction.

Adding the Border

1. Referring to the Wallhanging Top Assembly Diagram, sew the light beige 3-1/2" x 37-1/2" border strips to opposite sides of the wallhanging center. Press seams toward the border.

2. Sew the light beige print 3-1/2" x 34-1/4" border strips to the remaining edges of the wallhanging center. Press seams toward the border.

Complete the Wallhanging

1. Layer wallhanging top, batting and backing.

2. Quilt as desired.

3. Bind with blue binding strips.

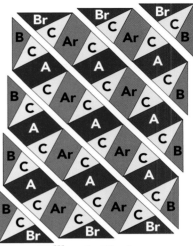

Wallhanging Center Assembly Diagram

Wallhanging Top Assembly Diagram

Cartago Table Runner and Wallhanging Templates
Enlarge 130%

1/4" seam allownace

1/4" seam allownace

C

1/4" seam allownace

A

B

San Joaquin de Flores Church

The San Joaquin de Flores Church is located in San Joaquin de Flores, Heredia, Costa Rica. Construction of the church began in 1864 with architecture emulating a neoclassical style. The materials for the stone block walls were transported by oxen cart from Cartago, Costa Rica, which is located approximately 37 kilometers away. After nearly 25 years of work, the church was completed in 1888.

The tile floors in the church caused some initial controversy. The donor of the church floor wanted it to be constructed of stone blocks. This controversy was resolved and neoclassical floor tiles were ordered from Spain, following the desired style of the church.

Much of the San Joaquin de Flores Church maintains the original architecture and has been lovingly kept up over the years. On November 12, 1998, the church was declared a national heritage by the government of Costa Rica. To this day it continues to celebrate religious services.

San Joaquin Quilt

San Joaquin Quilt

Finished quilt size:
68-1/2" x 68-1/2"

Finished block size: 6" x 6"

Materials

2-3/4 yards solid light beige fabric
1 yard solid dark beige fabric
2 yards solid black fabric
1-1/2 yards solid terracotta fabric
5/8 yard solid burgundy fabric
4-1/8 yards backing fabric
75" x 75" batting

Quantities are for 40/44"-wide, 100% cotton fabrics. Measurements include 1/4" seam allowances. Sew with right sides together unless otherwise stated.

Cut the Fabrics

Note: The medium and large light beige triangles are very close in size. To avoid confusion, keep them in separate labeled piles.

From light beige fabric, cut:

- 4—5-3/4" x 42" strips.
  From the strips, cut:
  25—5-3/4" squares. Cut each square diagonally in an X for a total of 100 large triangles for outer border.
- 8—3-7/8" x 42" strips.
  From the strips, cut:
  72—3-7/8" squares. Cut each square in half diagonally for a total of 144 medium triangles for Block 1.
- 1—3-1/8" x 42" strip.
  From the strip, cut:
  8—3-1/8" squares. Cut each square in half diagonally for a total of 16 small triangles for outer border.

From dark beige fabric, cut:

- 6—3" x 42" strips.
  From the strips, cut:
  72—3" squares. Cut each square in half diagonally for a total of 144 triangles for Block 1.
- 6—2-1/2" x 42" strips for inner border.

From black fabric, cut:

- 3—3-1/2" x 42" strips.
  From the strips, cut:
  36—3-1/2" center squares for Block 1.
- 1—3-3/8" x 42" strips.
  From the strips, cut:
  12—3-3/8" squares. Cut each square diagonally in an X for a total of 48 corner and setting triangles.
- 1—2-3/4" x 42" strip.
  From the strip, cut:
  8—2-3/4" squares for outer border.
- 6—2-1/2" x 42" strips for middle border.
- 7—2-1/2" x 42" binding strips. Sew the strips together to make one long strip.
- 6—2" x 42" strips.
  From the strips, cut:
  120—2" corner squares for Block 2 and setting triangles.

From terracotta fabric, cut:

- 4—5-3/4" x 42" strips.
  From the strips, cut:
  27—5-3/4" squares. Cut each square diagonally in an X for a total of 108 triangles for outer border.
- 12—2" x 42" strips.
  From the strips, cut:
  144—2" x 3-1/2" rectangles for Block 2, setting triangles and corner triangles.

From burgundy fabric, cut:

- 1—5-1/2" x 42" strip.
  From the strip, cut:
  5—5-1/2" squares. Cut each square diagonally in an X for a total of 20 large setting triangles.
- 3—3-1/2" x 42" strips.
  From the strips, cut:
  25—3-1/2" center squares for Block 2.
- 2—3" squares. Cut each square in half diagonally for a total of 4 small corner triangles.

From backing fabric, cut:

- 2—38" x 75" rectangles.

Block 1 Assembly

1. Sew (2) 3" dark beige triangles to opposite sides of a 3-1/2" black center square. Press seams toward triangles. Trim triangle tails if desired.

2. Sew (2) 3" dark beige triangles to the remaining sides of the black center square. Press seams toward triangles. If necessary, trim the unit to 4-3/4" square. Make 36 small square-in-a-square units.

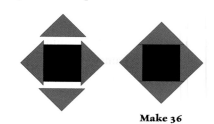

Make 36

3. Sew (2) 3-7/8" light beige medium triangles to opposite sides of a small square-in-a-square unit. Press seams away from center.

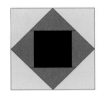

4. Sew (2) 3-7/8" light beige medium triangles to the remaining sides of the small square-in-a-square unit. Press seams away from center. The block should measure 6-1/2" square. Make 36 Block 1.

Make 36

Block 2 Assembly

1. Sew (2) 2" black corner squares to opposite ends of (1) 2" x 3-1/2" terracotta rectangle. Press seams toward the squares. Make 50 square/rectangle/square units.

Make 50

2. Sew (1) 2" x 3-1/2" terracotta rectangle to opposite sides of (1) 3-1/2" burgundy center square. Press seams toward the center square. Make 25 rectangle/square/rectangle units.

Make 25

3. Lay out 2 square/rectangle/square units and a rectangle/square/rectangle unit as shown. Sew the units together. Press seams away from the center. The block should measure 6-1/2" square. Make 25 Block 2.

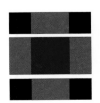

Make 25

Setting Pieces Assembly

1. Lay out (1) 2" black corner square, (2) 2" x 3-1/2" terracotta rectangles, (2) 3-3/8" black triangles and (1) 5-1/2" burgundy triangle as shown.

2. To make the left section, sew a black triangle and the 2" black corner square to a 2" x 3-1/2" terracotta rectangle. Press seams toward the rectangle. To make the right section, sew the remaining black triangle and terracotta rectangle together, pressing seam toward the triangle. Trim the triangle tails if desired. Sew this unit to the burgundy triangle, pressing seam toward the rectangle.

3. Sew the sections together to complete a setting triangle; press. Make 20 setting triangles.

Make 20

4. Lay out (1) 2" x 3-1/2" terracotta rectangle, (2) 3-3/8" black triangles and (1) 3" burgundy triangle as shown.

5. Sew the black triangles to the terracotta rectangle, pressing seams toward the rectangle. Trim the triangle tails if desired. Sew the burgundy triangle to the unit to complete a corner triangle. Press seam toward the triangle. Make 4 corner triangles.

Make 4

Quilt Center Assembly

1. Referring to the Quilt Center Assembly Diagram, lay out 36 Block 1, 25 Block 2 and 20 setting triangles in 11 diagonal rows.

2. Sew the pieces in each diagonal row together. Press seams away from Block 1. Join the rows together and press the seams in one direction.

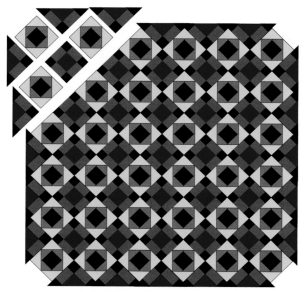

Quilt Center Assembly Diagram

3. Add the 4 corner triangles to complete the quilt center. Press seams toward the corner triangles. The quilt center should measure 51-1/2" square.

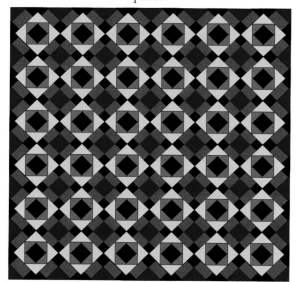

Adding the Inner Border

1. Piece the 2-1/2" x 42" dark beige inner border strips together into one long strip. From the strip, cut (2) 2-1/2" x 51-1/2" side inner border strips and (2) 2-1/2" x 55-1/2" top/bottom inner border strips.

2. Referring to the Quilt Top Assembly Diagram, sew the side inner border strips to the left and right edges of the quilt center. Press seams toward the inner border.

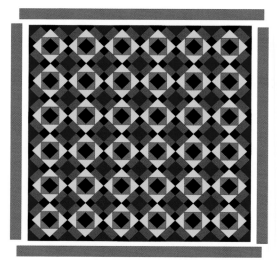

Quilt Top Assembly Diagram

3. Sew the top/bottom inner border strips to the remaining edges of the quilt center. Press seams toward the inner border.

Adding the Middle Border

1. Piece the black 2-1/2" x 42" middle border strips together into one long strip. From this strip, cut (2) 2-1/2" x 55-1/2" side middle border strips and (2) 2-1/2" x 59-1/2" top/bottom middle border strips.

2. Referring to the Quilt Top Assembly Diagram, sew side middle border strips to the left and right edges of quilt center. Press seams toward the middle border.

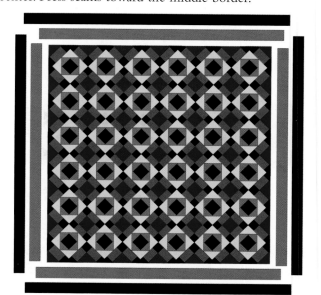

Quilt Top Assembly Diagram

3. Sew the top/bottom middle border strips to the remaining edges of the quilt center. Press seams toward the middle border.

Outer Border Assembly

Note: Refer to the diagrams with each step and the diagram on page 38 when making and adding the outer borders.

1. Sew (13) 5-3/4" terracotta triangles, (12) 5-3/4" light beige triangles and (2) 3-1/8" light beige triangles together to make a short outer border A strip. Press seams toward terracotta triangles. The strip should measure 2-3/4" x 59-1/2". Make 4 short outer border A strips.

Make 4

2. Sew (2) 2-3/4" black squares to opposite ends of 2 short outer border A strips to make 2 long outer border A strips. Press seams toward squares. Each strip should measure 2-3/4" x 64".

Make 2

3. Sew the short outer border A strips to opposite sides of the quilt center. Press seams toward middle border.

4. Sew the long outer border A strips to the remaining sides of the quilt center. Press seams toward middle border.

5. Sew (14) 5-3/4" terracotta triangles, (13) 5-3/4" light beige triangles and (2) 3-1/8" light beige triangles together to make a short outer border B strip. Press seams toward terracotta triangles. The strip should measure 2-3/4" x 64". Make 4 short outer border B strips.

Make 4

6. Sew (2) 2-3/4" black squares to opposite ends of 2 short outer border B strips to make 2 long outer border B strips. Press seams toward squares. Each strip should measure 2-3/4" x 68-1/2".

Make 2

7. Sew the short outer border B strips to opposite sides of the quilt center. Press seams away from quilt center.

8. Sew the long outer border B strips to the remaining sides of the quilt center to complete the outer border. Press seams away from quilt center.

Complete the Quilt

1. Sew the 38" x 75" backing rectangles together along one long edge, using a 1/2" seam allowance. Press the seam allowance open.

2. Layer quilt top, batting and pieced backing together.

3. Quilt the layers together.

4. Attach the binding to the outside edges to finish the quilt.

San Joaquin Quilt

68-1/2" x 68-1/2"

José Marti School, San Isidro

José Martí School is located in San Isidro, Heredia, Cost Rica. It was named in honor of the Cuban poet José Martí who loved freedom, independence and peace. The local neighborhood and education board worked with authorities to raise money and construct the school in 1928.

The school was built using the French construction technique bahareque. The mosaic tile floors have a Victorian architectural style. The tiles were produced locally in Costa Rica. The school is a mere nine kilometers outside San José, but is surrounded by mountains and farms. The building has been well maintained and expansions have been added over the years. The elementary school remains in operation.

José Martí School was declared a national heritage on March 23, 2007, by the government of Costa Rica.

San Isidro Wall Quilt

San Isidro Wall Quilt

Finished size: 34-1/2" x 34-1/2"

Block sizes:
12" x 12" and 5" x 5"

Materials

5/8 yard cream fabric
3/4 yard light green fabric
1-1/8 yards burgundy fabric
1/8 yard gold fabric
1-1/8 yards backing fabric
40" x 40" batting

Quantities are for 40/44"-wide, 100% cotton fabrics. Measurements include 1/4" seam allowances. Sew with right sides together unless otherwise stated.

Cut the Fabrics

Note: Label the fabric pieces and place in stacks as you are cutting.

From cream fabric, cut:

• 4—3" x 42" strips.
From the strips, cut:
32 large diamonds for Block 1. Refer to "Cutting Diamonds."

• 3—1" x 42" strips.
From the strips, cut:
24—1" x 5" strips for sashing and border.

From light green fabric, cut:

• 3—3-3/8" x 42" strips.
From the strips, cut:
28—3-3/8" squares. Cut each square in half diagonally for a total of 32 A triangles for Block 1.

• 2—4-3/8" x 42" strips.
From the strips, cut:
16—4-3/8" squares. Cut each square in half diagonally for a total of 32 B triangles for Block 1.

• 1—3" x 42" strip.
From the strip, cut:
12—3" F squares for sashing and border.

From burgundy fabric, cut:

• 1—2-1/8" x 42" strip.
From the strip, cut:
12—2-1/8" squares. Cut each square in half diagonally for a total of 24 C triangles for Block 2.

• 1—2-1/2" x 42" strip.
From the strip, cut:
12—2-1/2" squares. Cut each square in half diagonally for a total of 24 D triangles for Block 2.

• 7—3" x 42" strips.
From the strips, cut:
24 large diamonds for sashing. Refer to Cutting Diamonds.

• 12—3" squares. Cut each square in half diagonally for a total of 24 E triangles for sashing.

• 8—3" x 6-1/2" G rectangles for border.

• 4—2-1/2" x 42" binding strips.

From gold fabric, cut:

• 2—1-1/2" x 42" strips.
From the strips, cut:
24 small diamonds for Block 2. Refer to Cutting Diamonds.

From backing fabric, cut:

1—40" square

CUTTING DIAMONDS

Square up one end of the fabric strip. Align the ruler's 45-degree line with the trimmed end of the strip. Cut along the ruler's edge, creating a 45-degree angle. Place the ruler on the strip, aligning the inch-line for the desired width of the diamond with the angled edge. This will be the same as the width of the fabric strip. Cut along the edge of the ruler to make 1 diamond.

For this quilt's large diamonds, use 3"-wide strips and measure 3" from the angled edge to cut a diamond. For the small diamonds, use a 1-1/2"-wide strip and measure 1-1/2" from the angled edge to cut a diamond.

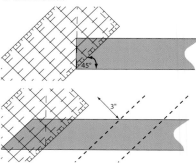

Block 1 Assembly

1. Sew 1 light green A triangle and 1 light green B triangle to 1 cream large diamond as shown to make 1 Left Point Unit. Press seams away from diamond. Make 16 Left Point Units.

Make 16

2. Referring to Step 1, make 16 Right Point Units, using the remaining light green A and B triangles and cream large diamonds.

Make 16

3. Sew 1 Left Point Unit and 1 Right Point Unit together to make 1 Corner Unit. Make 16 Corner Units.

Make 16

4. Lay out 4 Corner Units as shown. Sew units together in rows; press seams in opposite directions. Join rows to complete Block 1. The block should measure 12-1/2" square. Make 4 Block 1.

Make 4

Block 2 Assembly

Note: Block 2 is slightly oversized and will be trimmed later.

1. Sew 1 burgundy C triangle and 1 burgundy D triangle to 1 gold small diamond as shown to make 1 Left Point Unit. Press seams away from diamond. Make 12 Left Point Units.

Make 12

2. Referring to Step 1, make 12 Right Point Units, using the remaining burgundy C and D triangles and gold small diamonds.

Make 12

3. Sew 1 Left Point Unit and 1 Right Point Unit together to make 1 Corner Unit. Make 12 Corner Units.

Make 12

4. Lay out 4 Corner Units as shown. Sew units together in rows; press seams in opposite directions. Join rows to complete Block 2. Trim the block to measure 5-1/2" square, trimming evenly from all edges.

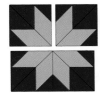

Make 1

5. Sew the remaining Corner Units together in pairs to make 4 Half-Blocks. Trim the Half-Blocks to measure 3" x 5-1/2", trimming evenly from the 3 edges with star points; do not trim the edge where the 4 diamonds meet.

Make 4

Sashing Unit Assembly

1. Sew 1 light green A triangle to the right edge of 1 burgundy large diamond as shown. Make 12 right units. Sew 1 light green A triangle to the left edge of 1 burgundy large diamond as shown. Make 12 left units.

Make 12   **Make 12**

2. Center and sew a cream 1" x 5" strip to the opposite edge of each burgundy large diamond from Step 1. Press and trim the ends of strips even with diamonds as shown.

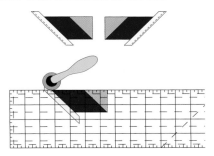

3. Sew a burgundy E triangle to each cream strip as shown. Press seam toward triangle. Trim cream strip in line with triangle to complete 1 Left Sashing Unit. Make 12 Left Sashing Units and 12 Right Sashing Units.

Make 12   **Make 12**

4. Lay out 2 Left Sashing Units and 2 Right Sashing Units as shown. Sew together in pairs; join the pairs to complete 1 Sashing Unit. Repeat to make 4 Sashing Units. Set aside remaining Left and Right Sashing Units for border.

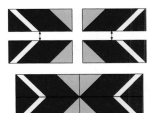

Make 4

Border Unit Assembly

1. Draw a diagonal line from corner to corner on the wrong side of 8 light green 3" F squares.

2. Referring to the diagram, place 1 light green F square on 1 burgundy G rectangle, right sides together. Sew on the drawn line. Trim 1/4" beyond the sewn line. Press open to reveal a triangle, completing Border Unit 1. Make 4 Border Unit 1 and 4 Border Unit 2 as shown.

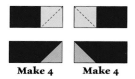

Make 4   Make 4

Quilt Center Assembly

1. Referring to the Quilt Center Assembly Diagram, lay out 4 Block 1, 1 Block 2 and 4 Sashing Units as shown.

Quilt Center Assembly Diagram

2. Sew the pieces together in each Block 1/Sashing Unit row and in the Sashing Unit/Block 2 row. Press the seams toward the sashing.

3. Sew the rows together to make the quilt center. Press seams in one direction.

Adding the Border

1. Referring to the diagram, lay out 1 Half–Block, 1 Left Sashing Unit, 1 Right Sashing Unit, 1 Border Unit 1 and 1 Border Unit 2. Sew the pieces together to make a pieced border. Make 4 pieced borders.

Make 4

2. Sew 2 pieced borders to opposite edges of the quilt center. Press seams toward border.

Quilt Top Assembly Diagram

3. Sew light green 3" F squares to the ends of the remaining pieced borders. Press seams away from squares. Sew to remaining edges of quilt center to complete the quilt top. Press seams toward border.

Make 2

Complete the Quilt

1. Layer quilt top, batting and backing.
2. Quilt as desired.
3. Bind with burgundy binding strips.

San Isidro Wall Quilt
34-1/2" x 34-1/2"

Encarnacion Gamboa School

Historically, the majority of Costa Rica's population has been Catholic. Almost all schools built during the late 1800s followed the construction of a church with the school being added later. The Encarnacion Gamboa School was unique because it was not tied to the construction of a church. The efforts of a teacher named Encarnacion Gamboa along with the support of the local community were instrumental in the school being built and open for classes in 1892. The original school had two classrooms, as well as an additional small building to house the principal and teacher who were husband and wife.

The building with the floor that inspired this quilt was built between 1936 and 1940. The design of the school was very modest and the tile floors were mosaic-style and handcrafted locally. The school has recently been remodeled and now functions as the House of Culture of Capellades. It is located on the outskirts of the city of Cartago where you can still breathe the fresh country air and take in the beautiful mountain scenery.

Encarnacion Gamboa School was declared a national heritage on July 11, 2003, by the government of Costa Rica.

Appliquéd Capellades Quilt

Appliquéd Capellades Quilt

Finished size: 72-1/2" x 96-1/2"

Block size: 12" x 12"

Materials

1-1/4 yards green fabric

2-1/2 yards dark orange fabric

3-3/4 yards dark brown fabric

1-1/2 yards total assorted
green print fabrics

1/2 yard dark orange print fabric

1/8 yard light gold solid fabric

Assorted gold-to-brown print
scrap fabrics

Paper-backed fusible web

1/2"-wide fusible tape

5-3/4 yards backing fabric

79" x 103" batting

Quantities are for 40/44"-wide,
100% cotton fabrics. Measurements
include 1/4" seam allowances. Sew
with right sides together unless
otherwise stated.

Cut the Fabrics

From green fabric, cut:

• 9—4-1/2" x 42" strips for blocks.

From dark orange fabric, cut:

• 9—4-1/2" x 42" strips for blocks.

• 7—3" x 42" strips for middle border.

• 9—2-1/2" x 42" binding strips.

From dark brown fabric, cut:

• 9—4-1/2" x 42" strips for blocks.

• 7—2" x 42" strips for inner border.

• 8—8-1/2" x 42" strips for
outer border.

From backing fabric, cut:

• 2—40" x 103" rectangles.

Block Assembly

1. Sew one dark brown
4-1/2" x 42" strip, one dark orange
4-1/2" x 42" strip and one green
4-1/2" x 42" strip together to make
Strip Set 1 as shown. Press seams
open. Make three Strip Set 1. Cut
the strip sets into 24—4-1/2"-wide
Segment 1.

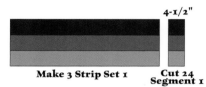

Make 3 Strip Set 1   **Cut 24 Segment 1**

2. Sew one dark orange
4-1/2" x 42" strip, one green
4-1/2" x 42" strip and one dark
brown 4-1/2" x 42" strip together
to make Strip Set 2 as shown.
Press seams open. Make three
Strip Set 2. Cut the strip sets into
24—4-1/2"-wide Segment 2.

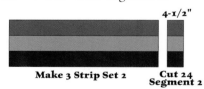

Make 3 Strip Set 2   **Cut 24 Segment 2**

3. Sew one green 4-1/2" x 42" strip,
one dark brown 4-1/2" x 42" strip
and one dark orange 4-1/2" x 42"
strip together to make Strip Set 3 as
shown. Press seams open. Make three
Strip Set 3. Cut the strip sets into
24—4-1/2"-wide Segment 3.

Make 3 Strip Set 3   **Cut 24 Segment 3**

4. Sew one Segment 1, one
Segment 2 and one Segment 3
together to make a nine-patch
block as shown. Press seams open.
Make 24 nine-patch blocks.

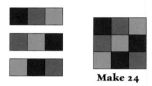

Make 24

Quilt Center Assembly

1. Referring to the Quilt Center
Assembly Diagram, lay out the
nine-patch blocks in rows as shown.

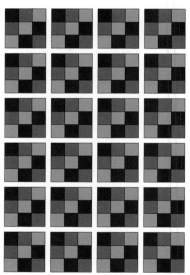

Quilt Center Assembly Diagram

2. Sew the blocks together in rows.
Press seams in one direction,
alternating each row's direction.

3. Sew the rows together to make
the quilt center. Press seams in
one direction.

Adding the Borders

1. Sew the dark brown 2" x 42" inner border strips together to make one long strip. Cut the sewn strip into 2—2" x 51-1/2" inner border strips and 2—2" x 72-1/2" inner border strips.

2. Sew the 2" x 72-1/2" inner border strips to the side edges of the quilt top. Sew the 2-1/2" x 51-1/2" inner border strips to the remaining edges of the quilt top. Press all seams toward inner border.

3. Sew the dark orange 3" x 42" middle border strips together to make one long strip. Cut the sewn strip into 2—3" x 56-1/2" middle border strips and 2—3" x 75-1/2" middle border strips.

4. Sew the 3" x 75-1/2" middle border strips to the side edges of the quilt top. Sew the 3" x 56-1/2" middle border strips to the remaining edges of the quilt top. Press all seams toward middle border.

5. Sew the dark brown 8-1/2" x 42" outer border strips together to make one long strip. Cut the sewn strip into 2—8-1/2" x 72-1/2" outer border strips and 2—8-1/2" x 80-1/2" outer border strips.

6. Sew the 8-1/2" x 80-1/2" outer border strips to the side edges of the quilt top. Sew the 8-1/2" x 72-1/2" outer border strips to the remaining edges of the quilt top. Press all seams toward outer border.

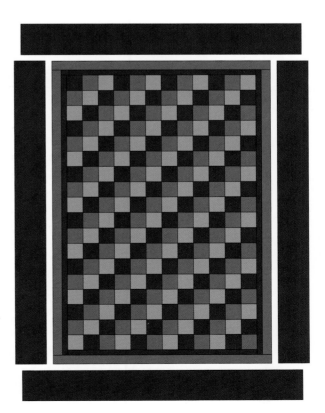

Appliqué the Quilt

1. Prepare the appliqué pieces using the patterns on page 51 and the appliqué method of your choice. Follow the manufacturer's instructions for using fusible web.

From assorted green print fabrics, cut:
- 1/2"-wide bias strips to total 540" for the vine.
- 90 leaves using patterns E, F, G and H.
- 90 leaves using patterns E, F, G and H reversed.

From dark orange print fabric, cut:
- 34 large flowers using pattern A.

From light gold solid fabric, cut:
- 34 large flower centers using pattern B.

From assorted gold-to-brown print fabrics, cut:
- 62 small flowers using pattern C.
- 62 small flower centers using pattern D.

2. Position the appliqué pieces on the outer border referring to the Appliquéd Capellades Border Placement Diagram on page 52 as a guide. Appliqué the shapes in place using your favorite method. A buttonhole stitch was used along the edges of each appliqué piece.

Complete the Quilt

1. Sew the 40" x 103" backing rectangles together along one long edge, using a 1/2" seam allowance. Press the seam allowance open.

2. Layer quilt top, batting and pieced backing.

3. Quilt as desired.

4. Bind with dark orange binding strips.

Appliquéd Capellades Quilt
72-1/2" x 96-1/2"

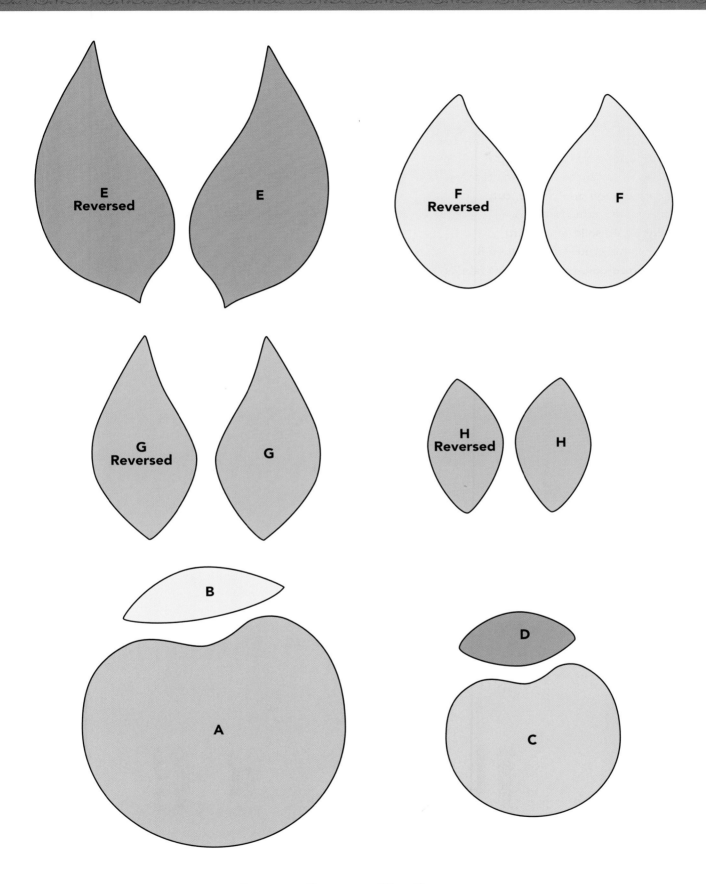

Appliquéd Capellades Patterns

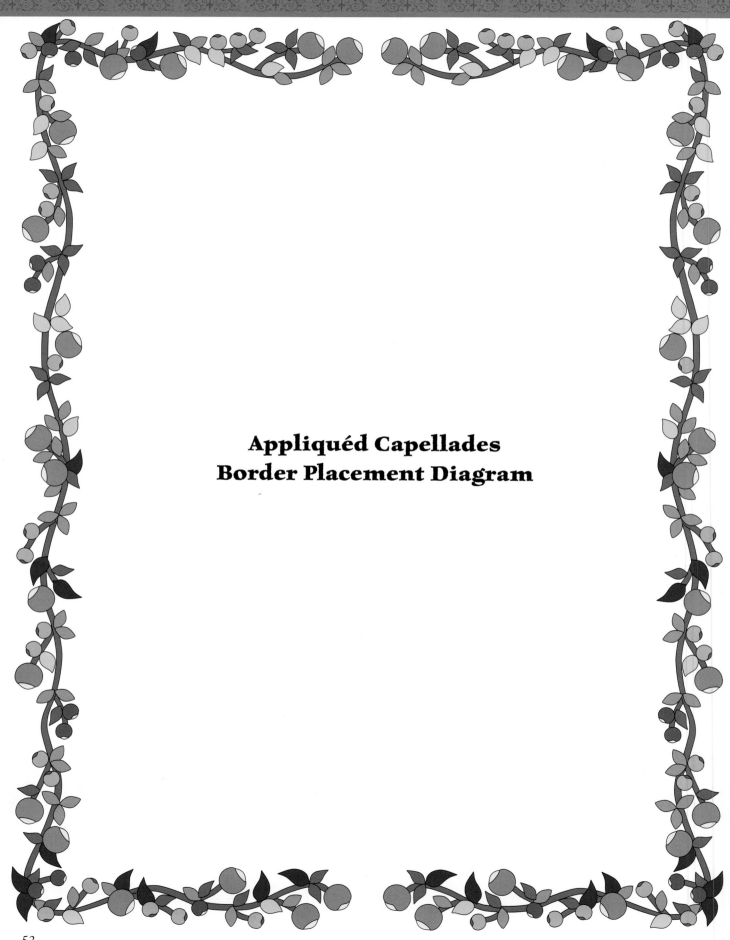

**Appliquéd Capellades
Border Placement Diagram**

Capellades Quilt

Capellades Quilt

Finished size: 45-1/2" x 60-1/2"

Finished Block size: 9" x 9"

Materials

3/4 yard burgundy fabric

1-1/8 yards gold fabric

1-5/8 yards black fabric

3 yards backing fabric

52" x 67" batting

Quantities are for 40/44"-wide, 100% cotton fabrics. Measurements include 1/4" seam allowances. Sew with right sides together unless otherwise stated.

Cut the Fabrics

From burgundy fabric, cut:

• 6—3-1/2" x 42" strips for blocks.

From gold fabric, cut:

• 6—3-1/2" x 42" strips for blocks.

• 5—2-1/2" x 42" strips.
  From the strips, cut:
  2—2-1/2" x 36-1/2" top and bottom inner borders; reserve remaining strips for side inner border.

From black fabric, cut:

• 6—3-1/2" x 42" strips for blocks.

• 5—3" x 42" strips.
  From the strips, cut:
  2—3" x 40-1/2" top and bottom outer borders; reserve remaining strips for side outer border.

• 6—2-1/2" x 42" binding strips.

From backing fabric, cut:

• 2—34" x 52" rectangles.

Block Assembly

1. Sew one black 3-1/2" x 42" strip, one burgundy 3-1/2" x 42" strip and one gold 3-1/2" x 42" strip together to make Strip Set 1 as shown. Press seams open. Make two Strip Set 1. Cut the strip sets into 24—3-1/2"-wide Segment 1.

3-1/2"

Make 2 Strip Set 1   Cut 24
                            Segment 1

2. Sew one burgundy 3-1/2" x 42" strip, one gold 3-1/2" x 42" strip and one black 3-1/2" x 42" strip together to make Strip Set 2 as shown. Press seams open. Make two Strip Set 2. Cut the strip sets into 24—3-1/2"-wide Segment 2.

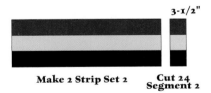

3-1/2"

Make 2 Strip Set 2   Cut 24
                            Segment 2

3. Sew one gold 3-1/2" x 42" strip, one black 3-1/2" x 42" strip and one burgundy 3-1/2" x 42" strip together to make Strip Set 3 as shown. Press seams open. Make two Strip Set 3. Cut the strip sets into 20—3-1/2"-wide Segment 3.

3-1/2"

Make 2 Strip Set 3   Cut 24
                            Segment 3

4. Sew one Segment 1, one Segment 2 and one Segment 3 together to make a nine-patch block as shown.

Press seams open. Make 20 nine-patch blocks.

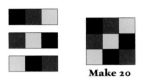

Make 20

5. Sew one Segment 1 and one Segment 2 together to make a partial block as shown. Press seams open. Make 4 partial-blocks.

Make 4

Quilt Center Assembly

1. Referring to the Quilt Center Assembly Diagram, lay out the nine-patch blocks and partial-blocks in rows as shown.

Quilt Center Assembly Diagram

2. Sew the blocks and partial-blocks together in rows. Press seams in one direction, alternating each row's direction.

3. Sew the rows together to make the quilt center. Press seams in one direction.

Adding the Borders

1. Sew the gold 2-1/2" x 36-1/2" inner border strips to the top and bottom edges of the quilt center. Press seams toward inner border.

2. Sew the remaining gold 2-1/2" x 42" strips together. Cut the sewn strip into 2—2-1/2" x 55-1/2" inner border strips. Sew the strips to opposite sides of the quilt center. Press seams toward inner border.

3. Sew the black 3" x 40-1/2" outer border strips to the top and bottom edges of the quilt center. Press seams toward outer border.

4. Sew the remaining black 3" x 42" strips together. Cut the sewn strip into 2—3" x 60-1/2" outer border strips. Sew the strips to opposite edges of the quilt center to complete the quilt top. Press seams toward outer border.

Complete the Quilt

1. Sew the 34" x 52" backing rectangles together along one long edge, using a 1/2" seam allowance. Press the seam allowance open. Seam will run horizontally across quilt.

2. Layer quilt top, batting and pieced backing.

3. Quilt as desired.

4. Bind with black binding strips.

Capellades Quilt

45-1/2" x 60-1/2"

Virgen del Carmen Church

The Virgen del Carmen Church is located in the city of Heredia, Costa Rica, approximately 12 kilometers from San Jose. Around 1823 the neighborhood community decided to construct the church to accommodate the growing number of parishioners attending La Inmaculada Concepcion de Maria Church, also located in Heredia, Costa Rica.

La Virgen del Carmen Church had a very modest beginning. It was constructed of wooden pillars, bahareque walls and a tile roof. By 1836 it was necessary to repair and whitewash the church to prevent it from falling into ruins. According to historical records an earthquake completely destroyed the original church around 1851.

The larger sister church of La Inmaculada Concepcion de Maria was also damaged and its repairs took priority over rebuilding La Virgen del Carmen Church.

Reconstruction on La Virgen del Carmen Church eventually began in 1861 and the architecture of the rebuilt church was inspired by Neoclassicism styles. A Cuban mason who used designs from abroad and raw materials imported from Germany installed the church's beautiful mosaic tile floors. The bright colors and design layout of the tile floors are a perfect complement to the magnificent oak pillars. The oak pillars were transported from the surrounding mountains by many oxcarts—a spectacular event itself. The reconstruction of the church took more than a decade. La Virgen del Carmen Church was inaugurated on July 16, 1874.

El Carmen Quilt

El Carmen Quilt

Finished size: 57-3/8" x 85-5/8"

Block sizes:

8-1/2" x 8-1/2" and 5-5/8" x 5-5/8"

Materials

2-1/2 yards beige fabric
1-1/4 yards light brown fabric
1 yard off-white fabric
1 yard rust fabric
1 yard black fabric
3/4 yard burgundy fabric
5-1/8 yards backing fabric
64" x 92" batting

Quantities are for 40/44"-wide, 100% cotton fabrics. Measurements include 1/4" seam allowances. Sew with right sides together unless otherwise stated.

Cut the Fabrics

Note: Label the fabric pieces and place in stacks as you are cutting.

From beige fabric, cut:

- 2—6-7/8" x 42" strips.
  From the strips, cut:
  10—6-7/8" squares. Cut each square diagonally in an X for a total of 40 I triangles for Sashing Units.
  Note: There will be 2 extra I triangles.
- 7—4-1/2" x 42" strips.
  From the strips, cut:
  24—4-1/2" x 8-1/2" A rectangles for Block 1 and
  7—4-1/2" D squares for Block 2.
- 4—3-3/4" x 42" strips.
  From the strips, cut:
  38—3-3/4" squares. Cut each square in half diagonally for a total of 76 G triangles for Sashing Units.
- 8—2-1/2" x 42" strips for border.

From light brown fabric, cut:

- 4—6-7/8" x 42" strips.
  From the strips, cut:
  19—6-7/8" squares. Cut each square diagonally in an X for a total of 76 H triangles for Sashing Units.
- 2—6-1/8" x 42" strips.
  From the strips, cut:
  8—6-1/8" J squares for sashing.

From off-white fabric, cut:

- 4—6-1/2" x 42" strips.
  From the strips, cut:
  24—6-1/2" squares. Cut each square in half diagonally for a total of 48 B triangles for Block 1.

From rust fabric, cut:

- 3—3-3/4" x 42" strips.
  From the strips, cut:
  24—3-3/4" squares. Cut each square in half diagonally for a total of 48 C triangles for Block 1.
- 8—2-1/2" x 42" strips for border.

From black fabric, cut:

- 2—3-3/4" x 42" strips.
  From the strips, cut:
  14—3-3/4" squares. Cut each square in half diagonally for a total of 28 E triangles for Block 2.
- 8—2-1/2" x 42" binding strips.

From burgundy fabric, cut:

- 5—4-1/2" x 42" strips.
  From the strips, cut:
  38—4-1/2" F squares for sashing.

From backing fabric, cut:

- 2—32-1/2" x 92" rectangles.

Block 1 Assembly

1. Sew 2 off-white B triangles to opposite edges of 1 beige A rectangle. Press seams toward triangles.

2. Sew 2 rust C triangles to remaining edges of the rectangle to complete Block 1. Press seams toward triangles. Make 24 Block 1.

Make 24 Block

Block 2 Assembly

1. Sew 2 black E triangles to opposite edges of 1 beige D square. Press seams toward triangles.

2. Sew 2 black E triangles to the remaining edges of the square to complete Block 2. Press seams toward triangles. Make 7 Block 2.

Make 7 Block 2

Sashing Unit Assembly

1. Lay out 1 burgundy F square, 2 beige G triangles, 2 light brown H triangles and 1 beige I triangle as shown.

2. Sew the burgundy F square, beige G triangles and 1 light brown H triangle together. Press seams toward triangles. Sew the remaining light brown H triangle and beige I triangle together. Press seam toward H triangle. Sew the sections together to complete a Sashing Unit. Make 38 Sashing Units.

Make 38

Quilt Center Assembly

1. Referring to the Quilt Center Assembly Diagram, lay out 24 Block 1, 7 Block 2, 38 Sashing Units and 8 light brown J squares as shown.

Quilt Center Assembly Diagram

2. Sew the pieces together in each Block 1/sashing row and each sashing/J square/Block 2 row. Press the seams toward the sashing units.

3. Sew the rows together to make the quilt center. Press seams in one direction.

Adding the Border

1. Sew 3 beige 2-1/2" x 42" strips together, end-to-end, to make 1 long strip. Repeat with 3 rust 2-1/2" x 42" strips. Sew the beige and rust strips together along one long edge to make Strip Set 1. Press seam open.

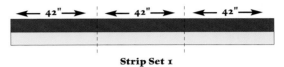

Strip Set 1

2. Square up one end of Strip Set 1. Align the 45-degree line of the ruler with the trimmed end of the strip set. Cut along the ruler's edge, creating a 45-degree angle. Place ruler on strip set, aligning the 3-1/2" line with angled edge of strip. Cut along edge of ruler for Segment 1. Cut 20 Segment 1.

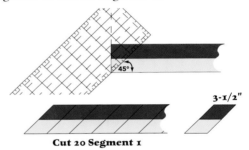

Cut 20 Segment 1

3. Sew together 10 Segment 1 for top border and 10 Segment 1 for bottom border. Sew the pieced borders to top and bottom edges of the quilt center. Press seams toward border. Trim border ends even with side edges of quilt center.

4. Referring to Step 1 and 2, sew 5—2-1/2" x 42" beige strips and 5—2-1/2" x 42" rust strips together for Strip Set 2. Cut 32—3-1/2"-wide Segment 2 as shown.

Cut 20 Segment 2

3-1/2"

5. Sew 16 Segment 2 together for 1 side border. Repeat to make 2 side borders. Sew the pieced borders to the side edges of the quilt center. Press seams toward border. Trim side border ends even with the top and bottom edges of the quilt top.

Complete the Quilt

1. Sew the 32-1/2" x 92" backing rectangles together along one long edge, using a 1/2" seam allowance. Press the seam allowance open.

2. Layer quilt top, batting and pieced backing.

3. Quilt as desired.

4. Bind with black binding strips.

El Carmen Quilt

57-3/8" x 85-5/8"

Thanks

A very special thank you to my husband Doyle. His encouragement, love, support and patience while I worked on this book was unending. He spent many hours on the computer working on the technical side of my designs so things would be easier for me. I could not have fulfilled this dream without him.

Thank you to my family and friends who helped and became such an important part of this project. Special thanks to my mother for teaching me to sew. Even when I was a child she encouraged me by allowing me to use her sewing machine and giving me all her fabric scraps.

This book is dedicated to my late father who always helped and encouraged me by teaching me to work hard for what I want. Thank you for that Papi. I love and miss you every day.

Acknowledgements

This book is the work of many people.
I could not have done it without all of you
Thank you all and God bless.

Ivan Serrano Mosaicos - El Castillo tile information
Arq. Ana Yancy Viquez - history information
Mario A. Sanabria - pictures and history information
Sandra Sanabria - El Baul de mi Abuelita quilt store Costa Rica
Coco Sanabria, Luis Sanabria and Sergio Vega
for driving me around to take pictures
Jeanie Rudich - Ye Olde Schoolhouse quilt store Cedarburg, WI
Mary Dorschner for her beautiful machine quilting
Rhonda Matus for her technical writing skills

Thanks to the Landauer Publishing team
for believing in and supporting my idea for this project.
I appreciate all the time you spent to make this book a reality.